Disrupting Healthcare

Blockchain Solutions in Medical Record Management

Table of Contents

1. Introduction 1

2. Unfolding Blockchain: A Primer 2

    2.1. The Genesis of Blockchain 2

    2.2. What Makes Up a Blockchain 2

    2.3. The Decentralization of Information 3

    2.4. Constancy and Immutability 3

    2.5. Blockchain and Healthcare: A Glimpse into the Future 3

    2.6. Transparency and Patient Empowerment 4

    2.7. Dealing with Interoperability Challenges 4

3. The Transformation of Healthcare: A Historical Overview 6

    3.1. From Analog to Digital 6

    3.2. The Dawn of Interoperability 7

    3.3. Health IT in the 21st Century 7

    3.4. The Emergence of Big Data 8

    3.5. The Advent of Blockchain 8

4. Significance of Medical Records in Modern Healthcare 9

    4.1. The Fundamentals of Medical Records 9

    4.2. Necessity in Evidence-Based Medicine 9

    4.3. Ensuring Continuity of Care 10

    4.4. Crucial Role in Preventive Medicine 10

    4.5. The Dawn of Electronic Medical Records 10

    4.6. Proactive Role in Personalized Medicine 11

5. Managing Medical Records: The Current Landscape 12

    5.1. Definition and Importance of Medical Records 12

    5.2. Challenges of Current Medical Record Management
Systems 12

    5.3. The Shift Towards Electronic Health Records (EHRs) 13

    5.4. The Role of Legislation in Shaping Medical Record

Management 14

6. Blockchain: The Catalyst for Change 16

6.1. Understanding Blockchain: A Primer 16

6.2. Blockchain and Electronic Health Records 17

6.3. Blockchain and Supply Chain Management 17

6.4. Blockchain and Clinical Trials 18

6.5. Regulatory Implications and Challenges 18

6.6. Summing Up 19

7. Real-World Applications: Success Stories of Blockchain in
Healthcare 20

7.1. Blockchain for Patient Data Security and Interoperability . . 20

7.2. Vaccine and Drug Traceability 20

7.3. Digital Identity Verification in Healthcare 21

7.4. Improvements in Health Insurance Claims 22

7.5. Conclusion 22

8. Technical Insight: How Blockchain Enhances Medical Record
Management 23

8.1. Architecture of Blockchain in Healthcare 23

8.2. Ensuring Data Privacy with Blockchain 24

8.3. Shared and Complete Records through Blockchain 25

8.4. Overcoming Fraud and Reducing Errors 25

8.5. Preparing for the Challenges 26

9. Legislation and Regulatory Implications: Navigating the
Blockchain Space in Healthcare 27

9.1. Blockchain in Healthcare: An Emerging Regulatory
Landscape 27

9.2. Addressing HIPAA Compliance in Blockchain Applications . . 28

9.3. Navigating GDPR within Blockchain Infrastructure . . . 28

9.4. FDA Regulations and Clinical Trials 29

9.5. A Forward-Looking Legislative Approach 29

10. Identifying and Overcoming Challenges in Adoption 31

    10.1. Technical Hurdiness 31

    10.2. Regulatory Impediments 32

    10.3. Poor Interoperability 32

    10.4. Scalability Challenge 33

    10.5. Perception and Trust Issues 33

11. Future Vision: The Forward Path for Blockchain in Medical Record Management 35

    11.1. The Paradigm Shift: From Centralized to Distributed Systems 35

    11.2. Blockchain Integration: Challenges and Considerations . . . 36

    11.3. Navigating the Change: Embracing a Blockchain Future . . . 37

    11.4. The Road Ahead: A Vision of Blockchain Empowered Healthcare 38

Chapter 1. Introduction

In this special report, "Disrupting Healthcare: Blockchain Solutions in Medical Record Management," we embark on an enlightening journey exploring revolutionary technologies transforming the healthcare industry. This report, which deciphers advanced topics in an easily comprehendible manner, highlights the varied facets of blockchain technology aimed at redefining rigid medical record systems. Success stories, technological framework, regulatory implications, and foreseeable challenges are all comprehensively explored with a keen eye on discussions. Rather than daunting you with complex jargon, we employ an approachable style, making this report an essential read for all those intrigued by the intersection of healthcare and technology. Go ahead and allow this insightful special report to demystify the realm of blockchain-based medical management, presenting you with a fresh perspective about the future of healthcare.

Chapter 2. Unfolding Blockchain: A Primer

The advent of blockchain technology has ushered in a paradigm shift not only in the way finance and trading operate, but also in how the healthcare domain is being redefined. At its core, blockchain is a distributed, digital, and decentralized ledger that records transactions across multiple computers. So, how does this redefine the healthcare landscape, particularly the delicate and important sphere of medical record management? To comprehend the unfolding of this revolution, it's crucial to understand the very basics of blockchain technology.

2.1. The Genesis of Blockchain

Invented by an anonymous individual or group of people using the moniker Satoshi Nakamoto in 2008, blockchain was initially crafted as the public transaction ledger of the cryptocurrency Bitcoin. However, its wide-ranging applicability and robust security offered a much wider scope, extending far beyond just being the backbone of a resilient, anonymous currency. It's the fluid and dynamic application of blockchain technology that has since caught the attention of multiple industries, including healthcare.

2.2. What Makes Up a Blockchain

A blockchain is made up of multiple blocks, where each block records certain transactional information. There are three main elements in a block: the data (transaction details), the hash (a unique code related to the block), and the hash of the previous block. This interlocking chain mechanism ensures that once data is recorded onto the blockchain, it's nearly impossible to change it without altering all subsequent blocks, making the blockchain system a much-secured platform to store and manage data.

2.3. The Decentralization of Information

One of the key components of blockchain that sets it apart from traditional ways of managing data is its characteristic decentralization. Unlike traditional storage systems where all information is stored in a single, central location, the decentralized nature of blockchain spreads the data across a network of computers or nodes, ensuring better security. This becomes particularly important in sensitive sectors such as healthcare, where the integrity of patient's data is of utmost importance.

2.4. Constancy and Immutability

Besides decentralization, blockchain also exhibits two primary characteristics - constancy and immutability. Each block in the chain carries a 'hash pointer' that refers back to its previous block, plus the timestamp and transaction data. This link between blocks is what keeps the blockchain consistent. On the other hand, immutability refers to the impressive feature of blockchain where, once a data is recorded in a block, it cannot be edited, deleted, or tampered with. This feature hugely amplifies the security aspect of data handling.

2.5. Blockchain and Healthcare: A Glimpse into the Future

With the general overview of what blockchain is, it's easier to connect the dots and comprehend how healthcare stands to benefit from this technological revolution. For instance, a patient's medicinal history, doctor visitations, treatment records, and billing details can all be stored securely in a blockchain, offering the potential for seamless, secure data transmission.

2.6. Transparency and Patient Empowerment

One of the significant advantages of implementing blockchain in healthcare is the high degree of transparency it delivers. Given its mutually verified and immutable nature, blockchain not only prevents any fraudulent activities but also empowers patients by giving them ultimate control of their data. They can decide who has access to their data, and for what purpose, giving them an unprecedented level of control over their personal medical information.

2.7. Dealing with Interoperability Challenges

Blockchain can potentially solve the persistent issue of interoperability— effectively communicating and exchanging data between different health information systems and software applications— in the healthcare industry. By providing an integrated and standardized system, blockchain eliminates the possibility of inconsistencies and duplication, often seen in the healthcare databases.

To conclude, blockchain technology, owing to its many exceptional features, could indeed be the panacea for the persistent issues around medical record management. It not only promises enhanced security and data protection but also patient empowerment and interoperability. However, utilizing blockchain technology optimally and integrating it into the existing healthcare framework does present its set of challenges and considerations, which we will delve into in the upcoming sections. This chapter certainly marks the first step in comprehending the potential revolutionary transformation that the amalgamation of healthcare and blockchain technology holds for the future.

Chapter 3. The Transformation of Healthcare: A Historical Overview

The management and processing of healthcare data have drastically evolved in tandem with technological advancements, leading to transformative periods in the sector's history. The following narrative depicts these significant transformations, from rudimentary systems to high-tech solutions, preparing us for a comprehensive understanding of the application and potential of blockchain in managing medical records.

3.1. From Analog to Digital

In the earliest stages of healthcare management, when records were hand-written, maintenance, transfer, storage, and confidentiality were all tasks fraught with challenges and errors. The advent of digital technology, while improving these issues to an extent, also came with a new array of obstacles.

The transition from analog to digital processes in healthcare started in the late 1960s with the development of Hospital Information Systems (HIS). The early electronic health records (EHRs) of the 1970s rapidly improved in design and functionality, however, full digitization was still a far-off reality due to limitations in the technology of the era.

Early EHRs faced interoperability issues, restricted data sharing, and limited storage capacity, chiefly due to the absence of standardized data formats and the costly, complex IT infrastructure required. Furthermore, these systems were often too complex for the average healthcare professional to use efficiently.

3.2. The Dawn of Interoperability

As technology progressed and integration became an essential consideration, health information exchange (HIE) emerged as a way to enhance collaboration among different healthcare entities. This transferral of health-related information was primarily dictated by the need for seamless, real-time access to patient histories, enabling medical professionals to make more informed decisions.

In the late 1980s, interoperable systems became a significant focus in health IT, driven by the development of Regional Health Information Organizations (RHIOs), which assumed responsibility for sharing health information among different entities within specific geographic areas.

However, despite advances in interoperability, inefficiencies in securing sensitive data, high costs of maintaining infrastructures, and the continued absence of universally accepted standardization hampered the growth and effectiveness of these systems.

3.3. Health IT in the 21st Century

The new millennium brought about a shift in health IT, underpinned by the adoption of EHRs. The Health Information Technology for Economic and Clinical Health (HITECH) Act in 2009 prompted this leap, allotting funds for EHR implementation and incentivizing providers to demonstrate meaningful use of EHRs.

Despite the widespread adoption and standardization of EHRs, new challenges arose. These include an increase in data breaches, the lack of comprehensive data-sharing due to vendor lock-in, the persistence of paper documents in some parts of the system, and high costs related to achieving interoperability.

3.4. The Emergence of Big Data

The contemporary healthcare landscape is being transformed by big data. This vast volume of complex data is brought about by a myriad of sources such as EHRs, wearable devices, genome sequencing, and social media. The transition to value-based care, powered by data science and predictive analytics, has seen healthcare providers rely more on big data to improve patient outcomes while reducing costs.

However, this data revolution has ushered in further challenges, including infrastructure and storage problems, data security, privacy concerns, and the need for advanced data analytics capabilities and streamlined data governance.

3.5. The Advent of Blockchain

The escalating complexities linked to data management in healthcare herald the advent of blockchain technology. Its ability to offer secure, immutable, interoperable, and trustless transactions makes it a promising solution for many of the aforementioned problems. Blockchain's potential for creating decentralized, patient-centric health data exchanges where data privacy is preserved provides a silver lining for what could be the next significant transformation in healthcare.

All these epochs of healthcare transformation have built the foundation for the rise of blockchain in healthcare. The journey traversed so far has pushed limits, opened new territories, and continues to innovate in the quest for the optimal solution to healthcare's complex problem of managing and using data.

We will delve deeper into the nitty-gritty of blockchain in the upcoming sections, dissecting the technology's potential in disrupting the current healthcare paradigm, with a particular focus on medical record management.

Chapter 4. Significance of Medical Records in Modern Healthcare

Medical records are the lifeblood of the healthcare industry, serving as a testament to the evolution of patient care and embodying the core of clinical decision-making. Each record, a mosaic of information, is crucial in determining optimum treatment protocols, and their importance in the contemporary healthcare sector cannot be overstated.

4.1. The Fundamentals of Medical Records

Contrary to popular perception, a patient's medical record is not a single document. Instead, it acts as a comprehensive repository of all health-related data gathered over the course of an individual's health journey. The record encompasses everything from examination results, symptom descriptions, medical histories, allergies, medications, lab reports, diagnostic images, and treatment plans. The assembled data furnishes healthcare professionals with a detailed record of a patient's health and disease progression, informing diagnostic and therapeutic decisions.

4.2. Necessity in Evidence-Based Medicine

In an era where evidence-based medicine is gaining prominence, medical records form the cornerstone of this pragmatic approach. By enabling professionals to analyze past treatments and their outcomes objectively, medical records foster the continual improvement of healthcare quality. This includes double-checking previous diagnostic processes, reassessing patient progress, verifying billing information, and offering data to be utilized for population health studies and biomedical research. They are also vital for medico-legal purposes, serving as irrefutable evidence in the event of legal inquiries or disputes.

4.3. Ensuring Continuity of Care

One of the fundamental characteristics of modern healthcare is the interdisciplinary nature of care provision. A patient might engage with several healthcare professionals, each specialized in different domains. Medical records ensure continuity of care by providing each new specialist with a precise overview of past diagnoses, treatments, and therapeutic responses.

4.4. Crucial Role in Preventive Medicine

With the uprising of preventive medicine, medical records hold a decisive role. A well-maintained record assists in predicting potential health risks based on individual and familial medical history. Regular screenings, immunizations, lifestyle modifications can be advised considerably more accurately, hence championing the cause of preventive healthcare.

4.5. The Dawn of Electronic Medical Records

In the digital age, medical records have transcended the archaic realms of paper and ink. Electronic medical records (EMRs) have streamlined and revolutionized care by making health data instantly accessible to healthcare professionals across locations. A digital approach, however, is not without its limitations. These include concerns related to data privacy, security, interoperability.

4.6. Proactive Role in Personalized Medicine

With the emergence of personalized medicine, the medical record of the future is likely to contain much more than traditional health information. Soon, it could include the patient's genetic profile, monitoring data from wearable devices, social factors influencing health and so on. This enlarged perspective would ameliorate the prediction and prevention of diseases, addressing them at a fundamentally individual level.

In conclusion, medical records are the lynchpin in contemporary healthcare, extending beyond the scope of patient care to influence public health, research, and policy. Their efficient management is fundamental to ensuring qualitative and secure healthcare. The advent of blockchain technologies stands poised to redefine medical record management, addressing various challenges while promoting transparency and trust. Much like in other sectors, the intersection of healthcare and technology is driving unprecedented change, ushering us into a new era of medical innovation.

Please note that the capabilities, potential, and limitations of blockchain technology as it impacts medical record management will be delved into in subsequent sections of this report. This includes investigating the potential that blockchain holds for elevating the standard of medical record management, serving as a backbone for secure, interoperable, patient-centric health systems. Such discussions will also offer insights into the experiences of those organizations which have already begun to explore this exciting digital frontier.

Chapter 5. Managing Medical Records: The Current Landscape

Healthcare is a complex system marked by several intertwined paradigms. Among these, the management of medical records remains a challenging area. This task involves numerous processes where digital technologies can intervene to simplify operations while ensuring security, privacy, and efficiency.

5.1. Definition and Importance of Medical Records

A medical record is a systematic documentation of a patient's medical history and care across time within one particular health care provider's jurisdiction. It comprises a person's health conditions, symptoms, diagnostic tests, treatment plans, outcomes, and so forth. These records serve as a crucial tool in providing a comprehensive assessment that aids health professionals in making informed decisions to deliver effective and efficient patient care.

Medical records are the backbone of all healthcare services, aiding multiple stakeholders, including physicians, patients, insurance companies, researchers, and state health departments. They facilitate smooth operations and can significantly impact patient care and services, efficiency, and financial health of the healthcare providers.

5.2. Challenges of Current Medical Record Management Systems

These traditional systems of medical record management, though useful, come with their share of limitations and challenges. Fragmentation, interoperability, security, and privacy are fundamentally the four significant problems encountered in managing medical records today.

Fragmentation: Healthcare information often exists in fragmented silos within systems. Medical data can stretch across primary care physicians, specialists, labs, pharmacies, and hospitals, leading to incomplete or disjointed patient records.

Interoperability: The lack of widespread interoperability among different systems is a massive barrier to streamlining information exchange. Given the multitude of systems in use, the lack of uniform data standards is a persisting issue, delaying care and increasing costs.

Security and Privacy: The storage and exchange of data make medical records susceptible to breaches and unauthorized use. It poses significant concerns for the security and privacy of patient information, especially with the expansion of telemedicine and digital health applications.

Cost: Despite advancements, the cost of upgrading legacy systems or integrating new digital health solutions remains high, a barrier for many healthcare providers, especially those operating in rural or less affluent areas.

5.3. The Shift Towards Electronic Health Records (EHRs)

To counter these challenges, healthcare has yet made another shift from paper-based records to Electronic Health Records (EHRs). EHRs are real-time, digital versions of patient charts. They contain patients' medical histories, diagnoses, medications, treatment plans, immunization dates, radiological images, and laboratory test results in order to provide a comprehensive view of a patient's care.

Despite offering numerous benefits like higher quality care, point-and-click access to patient records, practice efficiencies, reduced paperwork, and lower healthcare costs, EHRs have not fully solved the medical record management problems. Interoperability, data security, and privacy issues continue to vex the system.

5.4. The Role of Legislation in Shaping Medical Record Management

In the US, the Health Information Technology for Economic and Clinical Health (HITECH) Act has played a significant role in shaping the landscape of medical record management. Passed in 2009, the act encouraged healthcare providers to show "meaningful use" of EHRs through incentives. However, it was not until the introduction of the Medicare Access and CHIP Reauthorization Act (MACRA) in 2015, which overhauled the "meaningful use" concept, that real progress was made.

MACRA subdivided the former "meaningful use" program into categories including Quality, Advancing Care Information (ACI), and Improvement Activities (IA). It motivates providers to demonstrate improved patient care. In spite of regulatory promotions, adoption of EHR systems is still evolving, with new pain points emerging.

Because every country has its unique regulations governing health data, the landscape of medical record management varies from region to region. Developing countries, still struggling with paper-based record systems, face a more daunting task in shifting to EHRs.

In conclusion, the realm of medical records management is fraught with significant challenges – from logistical issues surrounding interoperability to security and privacy concerns that impact universal trust. Is blockchain technology the answer to these complex predicaments? The next chapters explore this potential possibility.

Chapter 6. Blockchain: The Catalyst for Change

Before diving into the subject matter, it's crucial to establish a solid grip on the blockchain's fundamental mechanics. Blockchain is a decentralized ledger system that records and verifies transactions of value, such as cash, property, or even medical records, in a secure, transparent, and permanent way. The very essence of blockchain lies in its potential to disrupt traditional setups and power structures, altering the way we authorize, verify, and conduct transactions. This area will explore blockchain's unique attributes conducive to healthcare transformation.

6.1. Understanding Blockchain: A Primer

We could liken the blockchain to a mutual distributed ledger (MDL), where transactions are recorded with a timestamp and linked to prior transactions. This ledger is copied and distributed across a network of peer computers (often referred to as nodes), with records verified by cryptography. And once added, it's nearly impossible to alter a record, adding to the technology's robustness.

Critical characteristics of blockchain technology include:

1. Comprehensive transparency: Each transaction is visible to all network members.

2. High security: Transactions are secured through cryptography.

3. Decentralized authority: Authority is shared, reducing centralized control.

4. Authenticity and non-repudiability: Each node can verify the transaction authenticity.

Now that we have a firm grasp of what blockchain is, let's explore how this technology could act as a catalyst for change in the healthcare sector.

6.2. Blockchain and Electronic Health Records

Electronic Health Records (EHRs) have become the central repository of patient health information. Traditionally, EHRs are maintained across diverse systems, making data sharing and interoperability a challenge. With blockchain, we can create a unified and secure health data platform where the patient controls access. Blockchain, with its inherent security and transparency, can reduce fraud, enhance patient privacy, and improve health data interoperability.

Here's how:

1. Sharing and interoperability: A common blockchain-based platform can improve health data sharing among care providers, ensuring each entity has access to the most up-to-date patient data.

2. Security: A permission-based blockchain can safeguard patient health data, addressing the ever-increasing concerns around health data breaches.

3. Provenance: Blockchain can provide an immutable audit trail, a valuable asset within any healthcare system to improve patient safety.

6.3. Blockchain and Supply Chain Management

In healthcare, supply chain management is a major concern. Counterfeit drugs and medical equipment constitute a significant risk to patient safety and public health. Apart from this, lack of visibility and accountability in the supply chain compounds the problem. Implementing blockchain can offer potential solutions.

Blockchain technology can track and verify every transition-point of an asset in the supply chain. Pharmaceutical companies can trace the lifecycle of their products, reduce counterfeit incidents, and assure the authenticity of drugs reaching the patients. By establishing a transparent and accountable supply chain, blockchain could minimize risks, improve care quality, and potentially save lives.

6.4. Blockchain and Clinical Trials

Blockchain could also profoundly impact clinical trials. Given that these trials generate a considerable amount of data, blockchain's attribute of providing a tamper-resistant audit trail can ensure data integrity.

Blockchain-powered applications can help monitor protocol deviations, informed consent, and patient recruitment in real-time. It could ensure the validity of the trials conducted, enhancing the credibility and reliability of the data obtained, ultimately benefiting the entire medical research community.

6.5. Regulatory Implications and Challenges

The application of blockchain in healthcare does have its fair share of regulatory and technical challenges. Regulatory bodies worldwide have yet to establish a solid framework to govern the use of blockchain technology in healthcare. Data privacy regulations such as HIPAA in the United States and GDPR in Europe, while essential, add to this complexity.

Moreover, there are several technical hurdles. Blockchain's

integration with legacy systems and ensuring it remains scalable as it accommodates vast amounts of data are among the challenges to overcome.

6.6. Summing Up

In essence, blockchain technology holds significant promise for the healthcare industry. While it's not a cure-all, its application could enhance various areas - from data management to supply chain transparency and research validity. As with any disruptive technology, the road to implementation comes with challenges. However, recognizing its potential and actively addressing these issues will pave the way for a more transparent, secure, and efficient healthcare sector backed by blockchain.

Chapter 7. Real-World Applications: Success Stories of Blockchain in Healthcare

Blockchain technology holds vast potential for the healthcare sector, from secure data sharing to more efficient patient management. The following real-world applications illustrate the transformative power of blockchain in healthcare.

7.1. Blockchain for Patient Data Security and Interoperability

Blockchain technology offers a practical solution to the challenge of data security and interoperability in healthcare. MedRec, an electronic health record (EHR) developed by researchers at MIT, uses blockchain to allow for easy, secure access to patient records across different healthcare providers. Patients hold the access control to their records, ensuring their privacy. They can also decide who to share their records with, allowing for improved cross-provider collaboration. This system mitigates the prevalent issue of data breaches, providing a secure health record management solution.

MedRec also provides an advancement in information interoperability. As the system is decentralized, all authorized medical institutions can simultaneously update and access patients' records on the blockchain, creating a chronological and tamper-proof trail of patient data.

7.2. Vaccine and Drug Traceability

Blockchain also has transformative potential in the pharmaceutical sector. FarmaTrust, a blockchain and AI-based pharmaceutical supply chain solution, uses blockchain technology to ensure drug authenticity and prevent counterfeit drugs from entering the supply chain. It assigns each drug package a unique global identifier which is tracked along its supply chain journey.

Not only does this provide manufacturers with real-time visibility and control over their products, but it also helps regulatory authorities to monitor the pharmaceutical industry more effectively. Counterfeit drugs can be identified and removed from the supply chain, and any illicit activity can be traced back to its origin.

With the COVID-19 pandemic, FarmaTrust successfully demonstrated its capability by ensuring the traceability of vaccine distribution. This global health event underscored the importance of blockchain in securing drug supply chains.

7.3. Digital Identity Verification in Healthcare

Blockchain has the potential to revolutionize identity verification in healthcare as well. Estonia's national health system is a striking example. Managed by the e-Health Authority, the system uses a blockchain-based identity platform that allows patients to control their personal data and provide access to healthcare services.

This system significantly reduces inefficiencies tied to identity verification. It decreases the time taken to access health services by eliminating the need for manual identity checks, leading to improved patient satisfaction. Estonia's successful implementation showcases the considerable potential blockchain holds for other nations' health systems.

7.4. Improvements in Health Insurance Claims

Blockchain technology can also revolutionize the health insurance sector. Change Healthcare, an American company, has implemented a blockchain system for revenue cycle management, allowing for the transparent and efficient processing of health insurance claims.

In this system, every transaction related to patient treatment is recorded on the blockchain, making the claims process transparent for all parties involved - providers, payers, and patients. This reduces the chances of fraudulent claims, leading to cost savings for insurance companies. The efficient process also leads to timely claims approval and increased patient satisfaction.

7.5. Conclusion

These real-world examples elucidate blockchain's immense potential in transforming healthcare. With increased adoption, we can expect advancements in security, interoperability, traceability, identity verification, and more. As these success stories illustrate, the future of healthcare looks promising with the integration of blockchain technology. However, several challenges - regulatory, technical, and ethical - still need to be navigated for widespread adoption. In the following sections, we will delve into these issues in detail.

Chapter 8. Technical Insight: How Blockchain Enhances Medical Record Management

The inception of blockchain technology heralds a new era in the field of medical record management, ensuring data privacy, transparency, and interoperability. It facilitates authenticating information and transactions, making it a tremendous transformative power for the healthcare sector. In this chapter, we accentuate how blockchain extends its robust capabilities to redefine the landscape of medical record management.

8.1. Architecture of Blockchain in Healthcare

In its simplest form, a blockchain is a type of distributed ledger that stores data across multiple nodes in a network. This sturdy and revolutionary technology ensures the highest level of security since any alterations in one block require consensus among network participants. In the healthcare sector, this translates into extensive protection against malicious attacks and data breaches.

A generic blockchain network in healthcare has the following architectural layers:

1. Cryptographic layer - This ensures data security and integrity using signature schemes.

2. Network layer - It allows peer-to-peer communication and synchronization of data.

3. Consensus layer - It verifies transactions and avoids double-spending.

4. Incentive layer - It encourages participation using rewards and penalties.

5. Contract layer - This includes the rules and agreements for the operation of the blockchain.

This multidimensional architecture, when applied to healthcare, proves exceptional. Each patient's medical records in the form of blocks link to one another to make up a chain. When a new transaction happens, it is timestamped and protected using cryptography, maintaining an audit trail and ensuring no unauthorized access.

8.2. Ensuring Data Privacy with Blockchain

Strict regulations like the General Data Protection Regulation (GDPR) and the Health Insurance Portability and Accountability Act (HIPAA) necessitate data privacy in healthcare operations. Blockchain's immutable, transparent, and decentralized nature caters to these regulations exceptionally well.

In the blockchain-based model, a patient maintains control over who can access their medical data. Their records never leave their possession unless they grant explicit access. This approach contrasts starkly with traditional healthcare record systems where hospitals and clinics act as custodians of patient records. The decentralized nature of blockchain ensures that patient's control over their healthcare data, ensuring their privacy and discretion are honored at all times.

8.3. Shared and Complete Records through Blockchain

The fragmentation and unstructured nature of medical records pose significant roadblocks to effective healthcare. Blockchain steps in to resolve conflicts resulting from fragmented records, enabling a seamless and organized system for health information exchange.

In a blockchain network, patients' medical data is right at the fingertips of the authorized healthcare professionals. The technology also enables a global health record system where patients' information from different hospitals and clinics globally can be brought together onto a single, consistent, and complete platform.

This holistic system allows doctors and healthcare providers to access a patient's full medical history, offering better diagnosis, treatment plans, and patient care. The absence of centralized ownership eradicates any territorial and institutional boundaries, thereby eradicating data siloes.

8.4. Overcoming Fraud and Reducing Errors

The records stored in a blockchain network are immutable, which means that once entered, the data cannot be changed or modified without the consensus of the network. This feature reduces the possibility of fraud or unintentional errors, enhancing the integrity and reliability of the data.

Human error is a significant contributor to discrepancies and inconsistencies in healthcare data. By employing smart contracts, blockchain can automate many tasks currently handled by humans in medical record management, additionally reducing the possibilities of error.

8.5. Preparing for the Challenges

Despite the multitude of advantages that blockchain presents to the world of healthcare, its implementation is not without challenges. Of primary concern is the privacy and protection of sensitive data, which are subject to stringent regulations in many jurisdictions.

Successfully integrating blockchain into existing IT structures will require concentrated efforts in terms of cost, time, and resources. Questions about its scalability also persist, as the technology has to handle a voluminous amount of data in real-time.

To conclude, blockchain technology is poised to overhaul the current systems of medical record management. It promises to streamline the process, reduce errors, improve patient control over personal data, and ultimately allow healthcare providers to better meet their patients' needs. Despite the hurdles and challenges at the moment, it is apparent that further research, development, and legislative adjustment will undoubtedly lead to the widespread application and success of blockchain technology in healthcare.

Chapter 9. Legislation and Regulatory Implications: Navigating the Blockchain Space in Healthcare

The race to transform healthcare with blockchain technology is gathering momentum, but it doesn't come without its fair share of challenges and potential roadblocks - paramount amongst them are the legislative and regulatory implications of this disruptive force. Despite these looming questions, however, blockchain's promise of enhancing transparency, efficiency, and data security in bespoke medical record systems is too compelling to ignore.

9.1. Blockchain in Healthcare: An Emerging Regulatory Landscape

The adoption of blockchain in healthcare poses various regulatory implications and requires a cautious approach given its nascent stage. Regulators worldwide view blockchain as a potentially transformative technology in healthcare, yet they walk a tightrope between fostering innovation and ensuring security and privacy concerns are adequately addressed.

Decentralization, innate to blockchain, fundamentally changes how patient data is stored and shared. This paradigm shift leads to new questions regarding compliance with existing legal frameworks such as the Health Insurance Portability and Accountability Act (HIPAA) in the U.S. and the General Data Protection Regulation (GDPR) within the European Union.

For example, within healthcare blockchain networks, who is

considered the data 'controller' and 'processor' under GDPR? Does the decentralization of data make it harder or easier for healthcare entities to comply with HIPAA's privacy and security rules? These are just a few questions among many within the emerging regulatory landscape for blockchain in healthcare.

9.2. Addressing HIPAA Compliance in Blockchain Applications

HIPAA has consistently been a yardstick for U.S. healthcare providers to measure their patient data privacy protocols. It is a comprehensive framework that sets the standard for sensitive patient data protection designed to protect individuals' medical records and other personal health information. Complying with HIPAA's regulations, especially concerning Protected Health Information (PHI), should be a priority for any healthcare provider seeking to incorporate blockchain.

While blockchain's encryption mechanisms could enhance data privacy and security, its immutable nature raises concerns about the 'right to rectify' PHI inaccuracies, which is fundamental under HIPAA. Therefore, exploring ways of ensuring seamless rectification of information on the blockchain without compromising its integrity is critical.

9.3. Navigating GDPR within Blockchain Infrastructure

Similarly, for the European region, understanding how to navigate GDPR within the blockchain's framework has become an important consideration. GDPR carries strict provisions for data privacy, necessitating a 'right to be forgotten,' which seems at odds with the idea of blockchain's indelible ledger.

Integrating GDPR principles into blockchain technology requires in-depth discussions around the core features of blockchain, such as immutability, data sovereignty, and decentralization. The dialogue should cover potential solutions like using off-chain storage for personal data, implementing advanced permission controls, or creating mechanisms to anonymize data effectively.

9.4. FDA Regulations and Clinical Trials

Apart from HIPAA and GDPR, specific considerations should be given to regulations such as those provided by the Food and Drug Administration (FDA) concerning clinical trials. When applying blockchain to store patient consent and clinical trial data, the system must adhere to FDA guidance documents around electronic records and electronic signatures, and more broadly, the agency's regulations for drugs and biologics.

The FDA has shown a positive outlook towards blockchain, acknowledging its potential to improve compliance, quality, and efficiency. Hence, aligning blockchain application with existing FDA regulations could hold potential benefits for clinical trial management.

9.5. A Forward-Looking Legislative Approach

Countries like Estonia and Dubai are taking a forward-looking legislative approach to harness the full potential of blockchain. These pioneer states offer a prototype of a favorable regulatory ecosystem around healthcare-focused blockchain applications. The rest of the world could learn and, possibly, lay down regulatory markers for the tech's widespread adoption.

In conclusion, a joint effort between technologists, healthcare professionals, and lawmakers is requisite to establish regulatory guidelines that embrace blockchain's potential while guarding against its risks. Bridging this comprehension gap will ensure that blockchain transforms the healthcare sector for the better without jeopardizing patient privacy and data security.

Chapter 10. Identifying and Overcoming Challenges in Adoption

The pivot toward blockchain technology in healthcare begs the fundamental question - what are the challenges that stakeholders might encounter in the process, and how can they be effectively overcome? As much as the story of blockchain's potential is a compelling one, it's crucial to assess and prepare for the hurdles that may lie ahead.

10.1. Technical Hurdiness

Let's start with the elephant in the room: complexity. Blockchain is a technological leap that incorporates an entirely new set of languages, concepts, and protocols, many of which can seem obtuse to those without prior knowledge or experience. In many healthcare institutions, there exists a lack of internal resources sufficiently equipped to understand, evaluate, and implement blockchain solutions effectively.

To address this technical hindrance, proactive steps must be taken. Establishing a core team of blockchain-savvy staff members within healthcare institutions could be an excellent place to start. Alternatively, third-party organizations specialized in offering blockchain solutions can also be leveraged. On a larger scale, policy makers and educational institutions can establish and promote blockchain training initiatives to generate a more tech-enlightened workforce.

10.2. Regulatory Impediments

Regulations in healthcare are rigorous and often complex, primarily to protect patient safety and privacy. It is not a space where disruptive technologies can be freely rolled out without stringent checks and balances. HIPAA regulations, data locality laws, and several other rules and guidelines apply to the handling of patient records.

When it comes to surmounting these regulatory obstacles, an intimate understanding of applicable laws is critical. Healthcare institutions must work closely with legal experts to ensure that blockchain solutions comply with the pertinent regulations. Notably, blockchain technology, with its inherent security and privacy safeguards, is largely compatible with the demands of healthcare legislation. It's about matching the technology with the legislative demands correctly.

10.3. Poor Interoperability

Information silos are distressingly common in healthcare. Different healthcare facilities and systems often use different terminologies, data standards, and protocols, making interoperability a significant challenge. The adoption of blockchain technology means the addition of yet another system into the mix, potentially exacerbating this issue.

Overcoming this challenge requires a concerted effort to ensure that blockchain solutions are built with interoperability at the forefront. Adopting standard data protocols and ensuring these are compatible with the blockchain solution will be key. It may also necessitate the creation of dedicated interfaces or middleware to facilitate seamless data exchanges.

10.4. Scalability Challenge

At present, most blockchain solutions struggle to scale efficiently. While the technology works well in smaller, more controlled uses, it often faces difficulties when the scale is increased. In health systems where thousands of transactions may be needed per second, this can be a substantial obstacle.

Solving the scalability issue may require a blend of technical and structural changes. On the technological side, pursuing more scalable variants of blockchain – like sharding or Layer 2 solutions – can offer potential solutions. On the structural side, considering hybrid models where only essential information is stored on-chain, with other data remaining in traditional databases, might be a useful compromise.

10.5. Perception and Trust Issues

Even though blockchain technology has come a long way from its humble beginning as the backbone of cryptocurrency, there are still various misconceptions associated with it, mainly relating to its security or the misuse of cryptocurrencies.

Overcoming this challenge is a matter of time and education. As more sectors start to adopt blockchain and more success stories emerge, public and stakeholder trust should naturally improve. Similarly, regular stakeholder communication, transparency about how the technology works, and persistent myth-busting can help to gradually shift perceptions about blockchain in a positive direction.

In conclusion, while the road to the widespread adoption of blockchain technology in managing medical records is paved with challenges, none are insurmountable. A combination of education, collaboration, adaptability, and a forward-thinking mindset can help healthcare institutions overcome these potential obstacles to successfully harness the immense power of this revolutionary technology.

Chapter 11. Future Vision: The Forward Path for Blockchain in Medical Record Management

There is no denying that blockchain technology is poised to disrupt the healthcare industry significantly - a revolution that holds the promise of transforming medical record management's current landscape. While the technology is in its nascent stage, it is indeed a promising tool for storing, securing, and sharing health records skillfully while mitigating concerns about data integrity, interoperability, and security.

11.1. The Paradigm Shift: From Centralized to Distributed Systems

The journey toward a blockchain-empowered healthcare system entails a transition from centralized to distributed systems. Traditional healthcare systems are centralized, meaning the patient data reside within a single entity, like a hospital network or a cloud storage service. This form of record keeping often leads to a series of challenges: data silos, lack of interoperability, data inconsistencies, and privacy concerns.

Blockchain brings a paradigm shift by propelling a swift transition to a decentralized system where every patient would own their health data, and healthcare providers can access them via permission-based protocols. This, in turn, nullifies data silos and inconsistencies and dramatically improves healthcare service delivery.

11.2. Blockchain Integration: Challenges and Considerations

Although blockchain is a potent tool, integrating it into the already complicated healthcare systems will not be a seamless process. The major challenges in its adoption swing around the axes of regulatory constraints, scalability issues, data privacy, and a lack of understanding and trust in this revolutionary technology.

+ Regulatory Implications: The adoption of blockchain in healthcare also comes with considerable regulatory implications. Healthcare providers will need to navigate regulatory barriers relative to information sharing to guarantee compliance with existing laws like the Health Insurance Portability and Accountability Act (HIPAA) in the United States. This begins with understanding these regulations and implementing mechanisms that ensure adherence to them.

+ Scalability and Performance: Another key challenge is to find a balance between public and private blockchains, each having its unique set of scalability implications. Public blockchains are anonymous and open to everyone, making the transactions more secure but also slower due to the broad participant base and high transaction volume. Private blockchains can process transactions faster due to a limited number of participants but may compromise data integrity and decentralization.

+ Data Privacy Concerns: Even though blockchain technology is lauded for its inherent data security, ensuring data privacy remains a substantial challenge, especially with public blockchains. While the transaction is encrypted and secure, the transparency of the system can potentially allow participants to see, and in some cases, link the data back to the individual.

+ Technology understanding and trust: Finally, the lack of understanding and trust in blockchain technology itself can act as a barrier. Healthcare providers and patients have to understand this technology's implications, which requires education and awareness programs.

11.3. Navigating the Change: Embracing a Blockchain Future

Despite the challenges, several steps can be taken to embrace a blockchain future successfully.

+ Pilot Programs and Partnerships: A insightful course of action is to incubate and encourage pilot programs. These programs can act as experimental grounds, where blockchain can be tested, refined, and integrated into existing systems without large-scale disruption. They can also foster partnerships among healthcare players, software developers, and blockchain experts, creating a comprehensive ecosystem for blockchain integration.

+ Regulatory Clarity and Compliance: For sweeping adoption, there needs to be a clear understanding within the healthcare community of the regulatory framework encompassing blockchain technology. Regulatory bodies must strive to create guidelines that are clear and conducive for healthcare providers to adopt blockchain technology without breaching existing laws.

+ Capacity Building: Concerted efforts towards capacity building, such as professional development programs, workshops, and conferences on blockchain technology, can help healthcare providers, patients, and policymakers understand this technology and its implications better, and build a sense of trust.

+ Tailoring Blockchain Solutions: Blockchain solutions aimed at medical record management need to be tailored to address unique healthcare sector needs. Innovation in developing privacy-preserving mechanisms or hybrid blockchains could allow us to mitigate privacy concerns and create a balance between data integrity and privacy.

11.4. The Road Ahead: A Vision of Blockchain Empowered Healthcare

The forward path for blockchain in medical record management is brimming with potential, pushing the bounds of how we view data security, patient empowerment, integrity, and interoperability. The blockchain-based healthcare system of the future will be one where patients have full control over their health data, enabling seamless, secure, and efficient sharing, thereby enhancing health outcomes.

While the journey to this future vision is certainly long, fraught with challenges to overcome and resistant attitudes to change, the endgame promises to be transformative. Blockchain does not merely offer solutions. It pushes forth a new paradigm that reinstates patients' power over their data, uniting disparate health systems into a singular, overarching ecosystem that is unshakeable in its commitment to serve the best interests of the patient. The future of blockchain in medical record management promises nothing short of revolution, blueprinting the path to healthcare's utopian ideal of patient-centric, data-secure, and cost-efficient care.